A WOMAN'S VERSE

by

Susan Ealey

Susan wrote 320 poems. Her plan in later years was to turn them into a book of verse that would show a woman's journey through teenage years to adult life; encompassing love, loss, family and the inner strength to move forward no matter what life throws at you. It was to be called 'A Woman's Verse'.

Susan would share these poems over the decades with her two boys. Who would listen with wonder at the story of their Mum's life. Tragically, Susan passed away before she got the opportunity to publish her journey into this book.

Her two sons, Marcus and Matthew, found the 320 handwritten poems in a large folder kept under a bed. They spent three weeks typing up each poem, shortlisting them down and choosing an order of verse that would show their Mum's journey. It was as if she was there with them, the poems allowed her sons to learn more about the mother they adored, and her words will stay with them forever. This is Susan's journey in 'A WOMAN'S VERSE'.

Dedicated to the memory of the most
beautiful and generous person in the world
(our Mum)

SUSAN EALEY
December 17th, 1949 – October 12th, 2019

Your words will now live on forever.
Eternal love your sons
Marcus and Matthew-John

VOLUME 1
Circles

Poems

You ask me why I write poems
And of my need to write
It's my kind of physicality
It gives me strength to fight
Each word that I write
Comes from so deep within
Fantasies, loves, desires, even sins
Each one is its own story, fantasy, love or
sin
Perhaps just a little of me is written between
each line
They are the stories of my soul, never to
age with time

Life Is No Rehearsal

Life is no dress rehearsal, listen when I say
For we are born up on the stages
To act in our own play

Each play we take part in
Is different from the rest
As though we are auditioning
For the final test

Sometimes we read our scripts wrong
And nothing goes quite right
With eyes in search for answers
But no one is in sight

We are left alone now
Insecure and lost
Forever stumbling on our words
We have to pay our cost

We must try to remember, before our final
curtain falls
To live each play with passion
And always give our all

Sweet Smell Of Youth

Oh, sweet smell of youth
Have you come to me again?
Like a beautiful rose
That blooms with rain

When you first feel longing at a lover's touch
The fire of passion I've missed so much

To look into eyes
And want each other so
The endless desires
Is like a river that flows

Though unlike youth, you can take pain
For you have learnt, love always comes
again

A Man's Life

If I'm allowed to be born again
I'd come back a man
For then I could achieve my aims
Do all I can
Men have life so good
Have their cake
And eat it too
They marry one woman
But never stay true

In My Prime

So here I am, a woman just starting in my
prime
The way my body needs to feel, really is a
crime

The girl has left my body
My mind is more mature
I know just what I'm after
But cannot find a cure

This new need for desire, filled with longing
and passion
As though I've opened the door to a whole
new world of fashion

Episodes that I would turn over so quickly in
my books
Now I've found I read more slowly, take a
second look

True the face shows lines,
That never used to be
For now, I am woman,
At last I can be me

Sold My Soul

I sold my soul to the Devil, one cold and
lonely day
He understood my passion, along to run
and play
Unknown passion I dreamt of, he filled my
every need
Each fast and easy, he sent before me
Succumbed to hunger and greed
When my time was over, he smiled and said
farewell
My soulless eyes have entry, as I follow him
to Hell

The New Suki

Hello world, come and see
This is the new Suki, or I should state the
original me
So long on the outside, with just a cool
breeze
At last I am a woman, longing to please

Don't ask me of times so sad and since
gone
Now is the future I just have to be strong
Yesterday I know so well, the pain still cuts
me deep
Sometimes the cobwebs stay around too
long, and prevent me from my sleep

Then a new sunny day begins, a smell of a
bright new Earth
Today I must begin again, as if to start from
birth

An Alien In The Crowd

I feel like an alien amongst the crowd
Don't feel the need to talk
Though my soul cries out loud

Have I been born at the wrong time?
Or perhaps it's me
I'm lost in time
My eyes just can't see

Longing for love
But afraid to let go
If I answer yes
I just might mean no

Lost and alone
Oh, forever it seems
My days become a shielded bad dream

Circles

Life goes around in circles
Though the patterns don't shape the same
Unpredictable like the weather
We don't need winter to feel icy rain

Yesterday my mood was right
To share your dry white wine
Now my passion is lost in the night
And that feeling was so fine

Though tomorrow if I want you back
Will you turn around and go?
Fate and destiny of welcome days
And answers we're yet to know

Lost

You are so far away, yet still so lost like me
Treading carefully with each footstep, the
cracks you know you can see

Your eyes are more aware now
You know those tell-tale signs
Being drenched in winter storms
Before your skin could be fine

Warm smile and open arms, they seem to
know your need
Though we can both see through, their
endless greed
So funny after all this time, you're still
constantly on my mind
Born in the wrong place, or just the wrong
time
You all have halos high above, mine just
cannot shine

All claim to be family, friends forever to be
Though speak a different language,
completely alien to me
Perhaps I'm just a loner, searching for the
truth
My mind aged with heavy burdens,
My soul still full of youth

I Am Woman

I am woman, come make me shine
Born to be sensual, whole and divine
With that right spark, to light my fire
I'll be your fantasy, if you woo my desire
Like a special rose, to be handled with care
I open my heart, my soul I will share

I Was Born Woman

You call me woman
Yet childlike with ageless youth
Only a daughter of Satan
Could hide the heartless truth

Somebody, tell me the answer
My mind is so confused
I can see right through disguises
I know I'm being used

Give me a faith to believe in
And I'll give all I can
I was born woman
Though can't compete with man

Insecurity

Insecurity is a painful thing
It starts outside and grows within
The graceful body that walked so proud
Now the head is bent low, the burden of
darker clouds
The lighter heart that sang within me
Now lowers its blinds and prefers to be free
The days pass but the pain gets worse
Will I ever be free from this curse

If & Why

The world is full of *ifs* and *whys*
And I don't really know if we did that
No, perhaps we shouldn't go

So many questions
Answers never told
Some will remain a mystery
Even when we're old

Friends who you longed for, though
frightened to say so
For if you once committed yourself, would
they turn and go?

All those times you wanted to, and wished
you did
Life is like Pandora's box, the answers
under the lid

The Devil

One day I saw the Devil, he beckoned me
his way
Come my lonely lady, be mine and stay
If you walk through this door, with me
pleasure will be yours
No more hurtful love affairs, no more
mundane chores

Life with me is passion and lust
Lost love and honesty bite the dust
Every day with me is an endless love affair
With flame of destruction burning
everywhere
Destruction rules the soul and mind
I have no need for beings who are humane
and kind

But why come to me? I heard my voice say
For I heard you cry out loud and pray
Not a prayer that God should hear
Only I understand your passion, hate and
fear
But what of love and eternal harmony?
Woman if you want these feelings don't
follow me

When We Were Young

Remember when I was young, and Princes'
ruled my dreams
Now my nights are shorter, life's not as it
seems

Romantic nights and flowers, are very rare
to find
It seems I've lost my faith, and fantasies so
very far behind

Do we grow older, to see life in a darker
shade?
Or can we see the shadows, fall long before
they fade

Freedom

Don't stand too close
I cannot breathe
If you ask me to stay
I might just leave
I'll give you love, friendship and time
My freedom I'm afraid is strictly mine!

Walk The Storm

Who do I reach for when nobody's there?
I long for arms to show me comfort and care
I'm in a constant storm and feel so cold
My soul is young
My mind so old

Walk tall, hold my head up
Though frightened I'll trip and fall
Don't forget my suit of armour
Enemies are so cruel

This web that's been weaved
It's so hard to break through
My spirit will drive me on
Until my grey is blue

Bring Back The Clowns

Where have all the clowns gone
Who used to make us smile
Like the old-time movies
Stars with their certain style

Life seems so bland now
Such very little change
Perhaps our world needs a shake up
To rearrange

My Disguise

The hard shell I wear, is just a disguise
If you dare come close, you'll see love in my eyes
So many years, I had to stand so strong and tall
Surrounded by haters, wanting me to fall

With you I feel my passion
So long its been locked inside
I am woman born of man
Here to live just a short time
So many dreams and fantasies
Though so many hills to climb

Alien

If I looked into your eyes would I find the
truth
Lost and lonely years uncertain through my
youth
Those who lived around me fitted the puzzle
so well
Knowing I was alien though only I could tell

Whispers, unkind glances, spiteful words
mixed with lies
Lending, bending, I gave so much to try
True I'm no angel, pure track records are
hard to find
I'm just searching for a warmth of the very
special kind

I Need To Fly

Like the trees that reach for the sky
So, my soul needs to fly
Like the birds that spread their wings
I need to expand to better things

Trapped like a goldfish in a bowl
I need time to save my soul
Love and passion will be my direction
How I need a love to conquer my affection

Glass Of Wine

Just one more drink
Well, it helps to pass the time
Another few sips of this heavenly brew
My mind will feel just fine

Wow, I feel so carefree
Leave the chores, take a rest
Just drift into your fantasies
Where you can do your best

Soon reality comes around, too quickly it
seems
Why can't we leave our familiar, and let
reality use our dreams

Follow A Straight Line

Look right, then left
Start again
If you look back in the desert
You'll never be sane

Just follow that straight line
Until you reach the top
Though if you stop and listen to strange
stories
You'll fall back and stop

Use your inner strength
For weakness is a sin
Scare your nightmare
For a new dream to begin

Walk A Mile

Is there a time I can really be me?
When I no longer need to walk a mile
To feel a little free

To awake each morning
Feel whole and content
Instead being like my overdraft
Underpaid yet overspent

To walk into a room
Proud to be admired
Instead of feeling like yesterday
Bus ticket old and expired

And to look into a lover's eyes
Forever to care
Not to live in solitary
Always to share

The Shadow

There is a darkness surrounding me
It just won't leave me alone
It seems to follow me everywhere
No matter how far I roam

I may wear a smile on my face
Then suddenly it's gone
Once more I feel so unwelcome
Like I'll never belong

It's like no other pain I've experienced
Of the physical kind
Though it's deep within my soul
It throws dark shadows across my mind

For now, I know the answers
Have I enough strength to carry me
through?
I have to close the door on my past
For me to begin a new

Our Days

Where have all the days gone
When I believed in love
I had such faith then
What happened to God above?

Did I stop believing
Or take the wrong road home
Though I may be young in years
I feel I'm fully grown

My hair was long and wavy
Then eyes shone a green and blue
Then disillusionment clouded my stare
Life seemed so untrue

It pains me so to act like this
There is no other way
I feel so afflicted
Acting in their play

I hope the signpost will one day point the
way for me
Until then I'll just have to wait 'till destiny
sets me free

Fate Is A Mystery

How will I know him?
How can it be?
Be patient my dear
Fate is a mystery

Mystery be damned I said!
It's just the same old line
You will say anything for silver
Make their sunshine

She threw her head back and laughed at
me
Her eyes they sang a song
And just as quickly as she came
Then suddenly she was gone

Ghosts

A ghost found my memory
And now haunts my mind
Showing visions, I want to forget
To leave behind

People I've grown with
I see in a different way
Reminding me of when I needed them most
They had their fun and play

Though this will be a new challenge
Erase them from my mind
Each new day I will take a test
Hoping I won't find
The shadows that rode me longer
When I least expected them to
Just to find a peace deep in my mind

Leaving

She stood there at the station
Suitcase in her hand
Wondering if they'd notice
Let alone understand

Accusations would surround her
And ears will surely burn
Now she faces freedom
At last it's her turn

So many years of caring
Without one selfish thought
Her child-bearing years
The lessons she once taught

Now she quickly turns back
As she slowly boards the train
Shutting the door to memory's
Wedding day and name

The song on the radio made her cry
The words just spoke her heart

Pictures

Pictures, coloured photos, that brighten up
the wall
Sad or smiling pictures, some short, others
tall

Their eyes all seem to follow me
Around the square shaped room
It seems like only yesterday
I had pictures, time flies too soon

I remember I used to lay awake
Just wishing they were real
If only he would kiss me
His lips on mine I'd feel

Funny how pictures can combine
With fantasies and dreams
Before you grow to realize
Life's not as it seems

Lesson Of Life

Life goes go on, yes, we learn from our
mistakes
We learn to tell the genuine, from the thorny
fakes
Each lesson like a chapter, depends on our
desire and heart
We each have to feel a flame, to make our
true start
The flames could be forever, or cold winds
could blow it out
Only life with coldness, we long to scream
and shout
Soon the page will turn over….

Drifting

Drifting, just passing
Can't bear to be tied down
When people out stay my welcome
I begin to wear a frown

I guess I'm alien in this world
Where no one needs to be alone
Friends only bring me burdens
I'd much prefer to roam

Love, ah, when it comes to love
I need to feel fire burn!

Rest A While

Oh, how I'd love to sleep
'Till night turns into day
Not caring what time it was
Or another lie to say

Problems would be rushed from my mind
Rest would make strong
Perhaps I could learn to love again
And feel the need to belong

My eyes would shine much softer
My lips have a ready smile
Just to find true peace
And stop to rest a while

Climbing Mountains

So many dreams
So many stories untold
So many lovers
Yet to hold

All those mountains
That once looked too high to climb
Now I can achieve them
And make them mine

The rough stormy sea
I once feared to tread
Now I hold my head high
And walk straight ahead

Feelings I once held
But afraid to let emotions go
Now I am truly woman
In control to let my time show

A New Land

Go seek another land
Now you are fresh and new
Touch the palm trees in the sun
See the sky so blue

Swim in the clear blue water
Feel the soft white sand
Make love in the moonlight
And gently kiss her hand

Each day a new adventure
A story in the past
Seed the flame in your soul
So, it will always last

Don't live in the Monday life
Which you so easy do
Know your inner spirit
Be yourself and be true

Melted Snow

The snow so white and damp on the ground
I open my door but hear not a sound
It seems my whole is standing still
I need to touch, I need to feel

A tear seems to creep through my bones
Like being trapped in a nightmare lost and
alone
Suddenly, sky lights, and the sun shines
again
The warmth ends my fear, and melts the
rain
Sunny days and skies so clear, with your
love forever near

Lay in the sand, swim in the sea
Our souls combined forever to be
No more rain, no endless tears
With your hand in mine, I have no fears

This is my dream
So deep in my heart
So long have I waited
When will we start?

Never Stop Believing

Never stop believing in your impossible
dream
It will brighten up your darkest day
Where rain clouds might have been

Any goal you can achieve
Just believe with faith and trust
Don't ever give in or fall
Or your dreams will bite the dust

At times doors will shut
Though look ahead, doors are open ajar
Never walk with eyes straight down
Always look afar

Oh, I know what I say
For I will achieve my goal

Different Shades

She walked from room to room
Trying to find a cure
Feeling no need for love or passion
Yet so very, very, unsure

Was she young or old?
Perhaps somewhere in-between
Travelling for the emotional road
Through every land unseen

Peeping from a window
Feeling alien and alone
Like watching life from another planet
Where feelings are never shown

She colours her lips
Like a shadow green
To shade her eyes
With her suit of armour for a safe disguise

Smiling at known acquaintances
Though feels no talk
Just a brief "Hello, nice day"
Head high, commences her walk

The Trouble With Men

The trouble with men, once you've accepted
their name
They think it gives them the right, to control
your passion and brain

You're the little woman in the home
Children buzzing through ahead
I wonder do they ever know
You'd rather be somewhere else instead

Woman so much taken for granted
With so much passion inside
Suddenly that look shines in your eyes
There's nowhere to hide

You are a newfound woman
So gracefully passed your test
Your handsome young lover you desire
For you today, he brings his best

Jigsaw Pieces

Have you ever seen a madman unhappy
and cry?
Or heard a new-born child speak cruel
words and lie?

I wonder if my heart will still long for a
soulmate, or will it fly free?
Will I always be a reflection of someone,
who is just not me?

I wonder if we'll ever find that wishing star
We left so far behind
I heard your name mentioned, my heart just
skipped a beat
Longing to close my ears to your words,
cannot face defeat

Skeletons

Too many skeletons in the cupboard
Unable to close the door
Just when I think I've succeeded
They push me down once more

Sometimes I do escape
And feel so fresh and new
Then dark clouds hang over me
Pushing away the blue

The past should be like a chapter
Once read then pushed aside
I turn away the things I love
I must learn to swallow my pride

I've learnt to late if someone loves you
They care not what coat you wear
They too are searching for a soul mate
To forever share

Learn To Wait

Why in this world do we learn when it's too
late
We let things go when all we have to say is
wait!
Listen to your heart don't be a fool
Pride cuts deep when you act so cool

You may believe you act the part, of a
sophisticated kind
But you will be the one, who ends up blind
Blind to desires, that should have been
yours
We should try to open, not shut out our
destiny doors

Pot Calling Kettle…

Why is it when women take younger male
lovers
They always get condemned
Funnily it's not by a woman
Always by our men

It seems to bruise their egos
When they see these younger males
I guess they question young men
Where older men fail

Or perhaps it's the woman,
that gives her cause to stray
Where once her part was motherhood,
now she can choose her play

Long To Scream

It's at times like these I long to scream
Though afraid someone may hear
Though the anger erupts deep down in me
My words won't seem to clear

Longing for silence
Tranquillity to mellow my darken thoughts
Feeling like a wild bird at prey
I'll suddenly be caught

For I have this spirit in my soul
That's longing to break free

Memories

Life is so very short
Yet heartaches seem so long
Yesterday answers seemed so right
For tomorrow they sound wrong

Eyes that shone a green and blue
Suddenly turn grey
A voice that casually said goodbye
Now cries for you to stay

A pretty face so flawless
Not one line in sight
Suddenly your older
In the darkness of the night

Memories you stored away
For once upon a time
Memory and visions closed
Unknown in your mind

Waiting for you to turn the key, till once
again you find
To find that memory strong and beautiful,
not one moment lost in time
They make your days seem warm…
…And move your darkness into light.

Magical Age

Youth is such a magical age
So many keys unturned
Today now is everything
Tomorrow is no concern

A different time, new fashion, a handsome
face
So few tears or silken lace
You fall in love so easily
Though broken hearts fade without a trace

Passion and fire a longing inside
A feeling so real and new
Your first love has touched your soul
You know the meaning of true

VOLUME 2
Baby Talk

Pisces

Oh Pisces are you the day at the sea
So gentle and mild can you be
Always dreaming about things, you can do
Yet now and again your dreams make you
blue
Such beautiful pictures you write and draw
An author or artist of great talent I'm sure

Best Friend

I have a best friend he is my younger son
Such a beautiful child, naughty, wise, yet full
of fun
Yet he understands when I have dark and
lonely days
Just want to be alone is what Garbo would
say
I understand Mamma and I love you so very
much
Oh, my darling son let me never lose your
touch

Photos

Please Mummy tell me a story,
One of how you used to be,
You know long ago,
Before you had me

For I've seen photos, yes, I'm sure it was you
My, didn't you dress funny, could it be true
Your hair was long and pretty, like a model in a magazine
I smiled and gently poked with him – "Am I an old has been?!"
Oh no, you're the prettiest Mummy in all the land
Why I asked do you look at me strangely, trying to understand

Well, those photos frighten me a little, seeing you that way
Mummy don't ever leave, please always stay

A Child's Innocence

A small child's innocence is a gift to behold
So much mystery a lifetime untold
Every day a new adventure and game
No two thoughts are ever the same

They believe in such tales
That once lit our minds
So many questions of various kinds

Their only longing is a mother's kiss
For too soon they are grown
All this they will miss

Have Faith My Darling

What will life be like when I grow to be a man?
Will I be tall and strong, achieve all I can?
I'd love to be a footballer or perhaps a singing star
Or perhaps sail the ocean to distant lands afar
Oh, my darling son you'll be successful in all you do
Just have faith in yourself to see each dream through

Baby Talk

Memories, sweet memories, of baby talk
Like pushing a pram, their first special walk
All those sleepless nights, their first tooth
comes to new
It may be cold outside, but they make your
sky blue

Their innocence, beautiful, handsome,
tiresome, but yours
They make a house-proud lady, easily
forget her chores

Oh, that newfound feeling
As they cuddle close to your skin
A warm kiss at night
Before another special day begins

Don't Cry Darling

Don't cry darling, your eyes will only look
sore and red
Anyway, by tomorrow, you'd have forgotten
what was said

I know when your young, life seems so cruel
and unfair
You learn as you get older, to love and
share

So much life ahead, yet your hurt cuts so
deep
Come rest your head on Mamma, I'll kiss
your wounds to sleep

Unborn

What happened to the child,
I carried in my womb
I took away its short life, it died too soon

Yes, I'm the killer of my child
I stand accused, I'm destructive, cruel and
wild
Oh, the decision I made, just had to be
There was just no way, I can't, you see

The memory will haunt me, as long as I live
For a child whose life, I never could give

Forgive Me

Forgive me my children
For outbursts and tears
These are just frustrations
At dark lonely years

Oh, you are no bane
You've shown me true love
Pure as the Heaven in a blue sky
Teaching how to love
When life is so cruel
Giving me strength
Making me stand tall

Sometimes regimental
Sometimes the clown
Watching you grow up makes me high
No darkness brings me down

I'm so proud to be your mother
Confidante and a friend
With each other we have no guilt
To borrow or lend

Love Mamma

Times Like These

It's times like these when I need your love
and guidance,
To see me through
You had that wonderful gift to change,
My grey skies to blue

When my crown had fallen,
You placed it back on top
You wore that beautiful smile on your face,
That made my anger stop

Ah, but now you are no longer here,
And I'm so alone
In my heart I'm still a child,
Even though I'm fully grown

I will try and be like you,
Wise and fall of grace
I'll pretend that you are by my side,
With a smile upon your face

Oh, my darling Mamma,
How I miss you so
Why did you die so young?
Why did you have to go?

I Love You Mum

This is the day you left us
With sadness in our eyes
Though you found peace and holiness
As you reached that unknown sky

It pains me to remember
Oh, why did you die so young
Long past chapters closing now
No new ones have begun

You are still my best friend and mother
No Heaven and Earth can take that away
Yes, I always feel your warmth
At the ending of each day

This is just a simple poem
Like I used to write you in the past
My love unlike words is never forgotten
Like eternity always to last

Love your
Susie

Strange Morning

Something felt quite strange
As I lay there in my bed
It was morning, time to get up
Though silence filled my head

Slippers on feet, I crept downstairs
Then suddenly I knew
She'd gone my Mother, best friend
Yes, it's true

Father just sat there
Tea shaking in his hand
His eyes searching for an answer
He couldn't understand

Clothes were all neatly ironed
Ready for us to wear
How could she leave us?
Told me she'd always care

I noticed the crumbled note in his hand
Then it fell upon the floor
Eyes red and swollen
He pointed to the door

Gone, she's gone
Just walked out not even goodbye
Said the waves were getting too deep to
swim
Lost too much to try

I stood there, too numb to speak
His words filled my mind
Then visions of her filled my head
Passing his words behind

I saw a woman still pretty
Filled with warmth and fun
Has she gone to seek her wishing star?
Or feel the golden Sun

Darling Mamma

Darling Mamma how I envy you
So far away up high
How I long to join you
Though I have no wings to fly

Down here is so empty
Just hate and deceit
Couldn't you plan a miracle
For us to have a meet

Since you've been gone, I'm so lonely
Burdened with a frown
People whom I once trusted
Have had their mask pulled down

I know I've responsibilities
A mother and wife
With this void in my soul
It's so hard to live my life

Just give me a sign you're with me
Cuddle me in my sleep
I'll have to learn to swallow hard
My tears will have to keep

Roses

Darling Mummy these roses are for you
And to prove my love for you is always true
My roses have bloomed on this special day
Even though you are far away
Though when I need you, you're here with
me
Mother and daughter, best friends for
eternity
Susie

Sunday

Another Sunday, another day
The same sharp words, and the children
play

Cook the breakfast, egg and toast
How I wish I was walking in the sand, near
the coast

Washing machine goes on, beds to be
made
These simple debts, have to be paid

Just once I'd like to lie in bed and sleep
Though who would attend to my children's
keep

In My Youth

In my youth I used to think life was just a
game
That any star was reachable for you to
achieve your aim

The handsome faces that I loved
Though fragmented to say I do
My freedom was growing strong
In my soul for me to stay true

Those endless stream of parties
To be seen at the best restaurant
I gazed with loving eyes at my friend
Though reserved, nonchalant

Marriage was a word that was alien to me
Though I craved pretty rings, I had to be
free
Then suddenly the wind of change, blew
around my life
I found myself without a world, mother, fool
and wife

Now the years have passed, all so quickly
so it seems
Though still deep inside, I crave, my
fantasies and dreams

Cheap Wine

You are that cheap bottle of wine
One drinks when ill
Aiming your knife at that desperate hour
When one's too weak to feel

Lose my temper
When my fire burns far too strong
I may have your name
Though to you I don't belong

Your sense of love and loyalty
Is your own paranoid sperm
With you I'm always on guard
I'll never surrender or disarm

Seeing now the winds are changing
There's a stillness in the sky
It's time to spread my wings again
For if I stay, I'll die
Not a death in lifetime, sense one of the
inner soul
You're without my sense of freedom, I
cannot achieve my goal

Daytime To Evening

The daytime is so good
But the evening has to come
That's when I want to shout out loud and
run

The washing of the dishes
Cooking all the meals
How I long for that taste of freedom
To know how it feels

Children are a gift that should be shared by
two
I've been solitary since before them
Now my skies aren't blue

Oh, to walk out the door, and find myself at
last
To look forward to a future, not drowning in
the past

The Dreamer

You call me a dreamer
No ambition to drive me on
In time I've lost my direction
With a desire to belong

Funny how it delights you
To ask what I've achieved through the years
Knowing I've been imprisoned
With past ghosts and their fears

You, well, that's another story
Travelled the world with drive
Me, I bore two children
With an inner strength to survive

Funny how quick the years pass, and winter
turns to spring
Time may have lived your fall
But your voice has a familiar ring

You'll Never Take Away, Who I Really Am!

You can claim my possessions
Or cloud the bright sunshine
You can tear chapters from my diary
Written once upon a time

Wash my face of makeup
With just rags to wear
Tell me I don't deserve love
Or I have no heart to care

Oh, to take away my freedom
Is quite a different case
For that would scar
Not even my mind could I raise

You ask of all those lost years, visions of
the past
I answer I didn't love him
Though our union seemed to last

Mistress

A mistress is such a well-shaped word, in
more ways than one
While the wife shares the children and
habits, she enjoys just fun

So, giving with a lending hand
When life's too much to bear
The picture he paints of his wife
Hard-bitten no time to care

She combs her hair, straightens her dress
Yes, the table's set just right
He rings the door, the looks in his eyes
Could you just once stay all night

The Evil Shark

Strange how certain memories haunt me
When my days were cold and dark
Of how you laughed down at me
You played the evil shark

With walls crumbling all around
It took every strength to stand tall
Trying hard not to listen
Kind words can be so cruel

How I needed someone to talk to
Wipe the tears away
Your so tied up in your ego
With evil thought at play

I never planned revenge
Or cruel ways to give you pain
I guess you sail many a stormy sea
Before you feel the rain

Now, well life's a little different
I've grown to be wise and strong
Though I'm still searching for the unknown
A place where I belong

People Say I'm Strange

People say I'm strange
With my desire to be alone
They call me the selfish one
For all the care I've shown

Accuse me of evilness
Like running up a debt
I wouldn't be surprised if they called
To come and collect

Oh, if only they could see
How my life's in disarray
So unsure of myself
Not knowing what to say

A Robot

The tears ran down my face
My head burns like fire
How I long to be in love
To feel passion and desire

I've become just a robot
Computers used, that's me
Wash and vacuum
I get the children's tea

Pretty clothes in the shops
I wish I could buy
I have a good imagination
And leave with a sigh

Places, friends, parties
I used to love so much
Now all I have disappeared
Like a lover's farewell touch

Incompatible

With you it's an endless nightmare
No beginning, no end
We may share the same name
Though you're not my best friend

Incompatibility, seems to rule supreme
Funny how first impressions, are not always
as they seem
You say one word, then act another
Claiming I'm ice cold, and feeling more like
my brother
You are ruled by ambition and ego, like an
endless serenade
With you I can't be woman, my passion will
only fade

The Alter

Do you promise to wear his ring?
Which will grow like your life
After cleaning dirty pots and socks
Will you still want to be his wife?

When he comes home drunk and amorous
Will you still want to feel his touch?
Will you ignore his passion for an old
woman?
Thinking you love him just too much

Before you walk down that long aisle
And kneel before the alter
As you hold your father's arm
Proud to be his daughter
Please listen to these words
Of a woman whose walked there before
If you can honestly answer yes
You must really be sure

The Dungeon

You locked me in your dungeon
So full of despair
When I needed comfort
You were never there

You were the first-class salesman
Your words seemed so true
Me being just a fool
Didn't see through you

Those dark chapters I heard, I shout them
from my mind
Knowing in my soul it's true, but kept pulling
down the blind

Then one day I found the key
Destiny had come to set me free
For in your world I could never be me

Even now you are trying to sell me a lie
No more can I hear you
I've paid my fine
Truly served my time

I Want To Be Free

I don't need you
I want to be free
I don't love you
You can't see me

All those days of loneliness and tears
Have made me a woman hardened with
years

My passion and fire
Is locked deep within
My celibate life
Which you condemn as a sin

I know someone, somewhere, holds the key
to me
Who will make me whole again, contented
and free?

Santa
(A Mother & Son Poem)

It was five past twelve on Christmas Day
The house was fast asleep
I pulled the covers down from my eyes
And dared myself to peep

Suddenly before my eyes
I saw Santa at my door
He smiled and said - "Ho, ho, ho"
But my eyes looked straight at the floor

Santa with no boots on
Just ten toes staring at me
He then looked rather embarrassed
And tried to explain you see

He'd got stuck up my chimney
Though dare not to make a sound
And his boots stayed there
As his body hit the ground

When my stocking was full
And we'd had a cosy talk
Santa said he'd have to find Old Rudolph
Or else he'd have to walk

Incompatibility

You condemn my actions
Call me the painted clown
Saying it's better not to laugh loud
Best to wear a frown

Your ambitions are so high
Always reaching for the top
Me, I'm just a dreamer
I need to look and stop

Incompatibility is a word I learned, I now
know, and understand
You are not my destiny, I'm not what you
planned

My fire is too strong
Your waves are too high
My only fear is drowning
If I don't swim free, I'll die

Friends

To be a confidante and friend
Is a price I dare not pay
They take away my freedom
With demanding words they say

Me, I'm a free spirit
Forever a butterfly
If I'm caged with emotion
I find a space to fly

I don't invade your privacy
Don't intrude on mine
Keep your distance from my haven
Don't crowd my life with your darkness
I need sunshine

Father

She asks puzzled questions
At your sleepless nights
Those endless nightmares
Which awake you in a fright

You dismiss each
With an answer that it happened long ago
Only you know the pain you caused
Though have no scars to show

Try to talk it over
For it helps to bare your soul
Where do you start with a story like yours?
You just might lose control

Only I know your puzzled mind
All that guilt which tears you apart
For you are locked within your nightmare
With a new dream to start

Destruction

I couldn't believe my eyes
That vision of chaos upon my floor
Swallowing hard, I tried to speak
Though held onto the door
All my entire past
Memories bitter and sweet
You had a look of self-victory
Mine was lost defeat
I'd only been gone a while
When he descended upon my room
Which was once full of childhood memories
Now such bitter gloom
What gives you the right to my cupboard
It was all before our time
You are my wife, your named now
These memories are not mine
I learnt so much that day
I now store things in my mind
For that is my only solitary
A place he'll never find

Marriage Long Died

My marriage long since died
And a heart that's near the ground
Answers, numbness, that's in my soul
With no lover's touch or sound

Yet still the woman bleeds
Just for a while you made me shine
And eased away my pain
I know this may sound crazy
I didn't know your name
Still the woman bleeds…

Yes, I can still feel passion
With so much love inside
Even with my baron soul
And all the nights I cried

I am born woman
We were made to bleed
Just like a precious rose, needs water to
grow
We need love to really succeed

Butter

You remind me so of butter
You just sit there and spread
Wicked thoughts fill my mind
Wishing you were dead

You speak in cliché pub slang
Humming between each verse
I wish I was a witch
With three cuts on you I'd put a curse!

Then you might try and seduce me
With hands that crawl and creep
I walk away, then turn
And hear you snoring in your sleep!!

In your bedroom I hear strange noises,
That would surely disturb a ghost!!!

Old Times

I heard your voice upon the phone
It made my blood run cold
The memories swept my mind once more
Of days when I was old

All those unhappy days
That turned into weeks and years
Days in my life when, my body shed
endless tears

You spoke to me words
Which you casually asked
I felt like a soldier in a war
Ready to fight a task

"It would be nice to meet again
Talk about good old days"
I heard my voice mutter – "Perhaps"
My mind still in a daze

Look I'm sorry, but I'm busy.

Trying To Stand

People can be so cruel
Call you the perfect fool
How little did they know
I tried to stand so tall

Everything around me crumbling, without a trace
I felt just like an alien, lost in outer space

You said you love me
Had your cake and ate it too
No wonder why I'm celibate
Turning away from you

True time can heal pain
Though the scars will always show
My only desire is solitude
With a wish for you to go

Moving House

Dear Father Christmas,
please make my wish come true
Make us sell this soon,
change the grey to blue

People come from near or far,
to snoop and look around
Me, I see through their smiles,
and their ever so pleasant sound

Either he loves it,
she says it's too small
I hate to stand and listen,
feeling the complete fool

A New Town

Another time, another place
A passing glance, a new-found face
Unfamiliar houses, a town yet to explore
Will I begin to find myself, or still feel so
unsure
Every now and then, past memories cloud
my mind
Now's the time to shut their door, if life can
be so kind

Fairytales

You are so full of fairy tales
Fiction to the core
Once making me feel inadequate
Self-conscious and unsure
Did I once believe in your 'Once upon a
time'?
Not seeing through your hollow eyes, saying
you are mine

When their words burnt my eyes
I pretended not to hear
It was then I built my own cocoon
To keep out hurt and fear

If warm new eyes dared look my way
I'd turn, never looking back
Always wearing a suit of armour
Ready for the attack

Then suddenly a strange new glance
A face I knew so well
Never before in this lifetime
Though past soul mates one can tell

Making me feel so high, so special and
brand new
You are my forever destiny
Our love is always true

VOLUME 3
A Song of Love

An Island

I want to be an island,
And made love to, like a woman should
Making me feel naughty,
While you make it so good

Waking up each morning,
Loving arms to hold me tight
I'll have no need to run,
Or use inner strength to fight

Just to look into your eyes,
Knowing you feel it too
Oh, if you could be with me,
And I could be with you

Valentines

Our eyes met across the room
I was captured by your spell
Whether other people noticed
I really couldn't tell
All I know, my only desire
Was to be held in your arms
Unaware of others close to me
Just mesmerised by your charms

Before I had time to catch my breath
You asked me for a dance
Unaware of the gossiping we were causing
Just in each other's trance

Then as the lights went out
We were just too close to part
What fate had destined and planned
Was just about to start

Valentine's Day is meant to be, of warm
loving hopes and kisses
One can also send a message, to the one
he truly misses
Unable to be together, fate seems to keep
us apart
Hoping this card will grant my wish, to make
our strong start

Asleep

If I'm asleep in a dream, with visions so very clear
Yes, I still love you, you know you're the only one
To think we are together after all this time,
And we've made our baby son

It seems a million years ago I was lost and so alone
Imprisoned by past ghosts and memories
Longing to escape and roam

I really thought I'd lost you, that cold winters night
Trying to unlock my passion, seeing I'd lost my stage fright
Oh, how I cried, it would fill endless rivers and streams
My only consolation was to hold you in my dreams

Romantic

The hunger in your eyes
The touch of your hand
You filled that missing piece of jigsaw
As though you had it planned

You spoke my name
My eyes filled with desire
Suddenly I found my destination
You lit my soul with fire

I truly thought a solitary life
Was to be my bane
Then just like a romantic novice
Into my life you came

You make me shine so young
But love me like a woman full grown
Just like a field at harvest
Every seed is sown

Velvet Tone

I hear your voice on my telephone
So dark with a velvet tone
You fill my mind with loving thoughts
A longing I've never known

We talk in simple words
But, oh, how deep they go
Time goes so quickly when together
When apart all so slow

You ask what I'm doing and the colour of
my dress
Telling me how beautiful I am, my, I look a
mess

Now it's time to say goodbye,
it gets harder every time.

The Music Is Wrong

You look at me, I sense you want to get
near
I long to feel warmth, deep down in buried
fear
You say I'm kind, beautiful and cool
Oh, that's just the surface, only skin deep
If only you knew my nightmare, where
reality is my sleep

So many faces that have come and gone
Each song the same words, the music was
all wrong
With you maybe I could go and get the
rhyme right
To walk the melody for more than just one
night

How Are You

Hi, how are you?
My, you look so good!
Looking at me with those eyes
Making me feel like I should!

Yes, it has been a long time
Since that very first day
When our paths crossed
And you cast a spell my way

Are you still searching?
Me? Oh, my puzzle is still incomplete
Or have you found your goal?
Longing just like me to fill completely whole

Tired with the worry of the day
I slept and dreamed you called me name
Sleepily I looked from the window
Though everything seemed the same
I lay my head back on my pillow,
and closed my eyes again.

Intimate Moments

To live life without you
Truly would be a sin
With you I'm forever at the crossroads
Unable to begin

I long for our lips to caress
To feel the touch of your hand
To feel each intimate moment
Just a smile to understand

You bring out my romantic side
The Monster cannot destroy
Together we could make a child
A beautiful girl or boy

If my fate is hand in hand with destiny,
that has so far kept us apart
I wish and pray to change that circle,
to make our story start

Our Songs

I'll write words, you compose a tune
Collaborate in harmony, oh, make it soon
Each verse will marry with your music so
well
Songs of eternal Heaven to soulful Hell
As each note is sung, we'll feel each word
and rhyme
Music and life, forever in time

Love Of My Life

Happy New Year my darling
Wherever you are in life
Me, I'm still the seeker
The house lonely wife

I wonder do you ever think of me
And our very special time
Remembering that very first look
And I knew you would always be mine

So many years have passed
With chapters I long to forget
Though to lose you the love of my life
Is a pain I'll never forget

Wavy Hair

How I wish I could see you now
With that smile and wavy hair
Even if I couldn't touch you
I show how much I care

I guess we'd talk of memories
And how it used to be
Before we both face the storm
High waves upon the sea

Would you still want me?
Or has that fire died
You never knew how I loved you
Or those nights I cried

It has been so long
Rules and years have kept us apart
Oh, don't you know it's only you
Who could make my story start

Crazy Valentine

Let me be your crazy valentine
For all the world to see
I'll be your very own circus clown
If you will stay with me

Every day will be full of laughter
No tears to cloud our sky
If you say you'll always be mine
I'll love you till I die

Goose Bumps

Sometimes I dream, that I'm being held in
your strong arms
I can even feel the goose bumps, thinking of
your charms

With you there would be no cold winds
Just a warm summers glow
Words will not be important
We'd just look and know

You make me feel ageless
Whole woman yet with a childlike grace
Oh, how your eyes love
With your handsome face

To Live Without Love

To live without love
Is living without the Sun or rain
Sun gives you passion
Water washes away the pain

A life without love
Is a rough and windy sea
Waves drown your affection
A windless struggle to swim free

You walk and talk with movement
Though something's missing deep inside
No matter how well your face paints
Your fear you cannot hide

Meet Now, Not Later

I don't want to meet again
When I'm old and grey, unable to bear fruit
Just take a look at me now
Woman, sexy and cute

My train passed through stations
Yes, I've been tempted by a sign
How could I take one step off
When my love is on your line

So, come let's find each other
True love never dies
Remember just like the first time
Such passion in our eyes

The Farewell

I wish you didn't have to go away
On those endless tours
True my lifestyle's so different
Never again to be poor

Though the daytime I'm kept busy
Oh, the night-time also long
You know I still play your records
I love to hear your song

The best times are when you phone
I fantasize you're here with me
How much I wish you would return
Then we could be free

I know it's hard for you having to smile
Always in the courtroom an endless trial
You know I hear stories of fun and games
you have while your away
This I know what all work did to Jack when
he had no play

But I know you'll always love me
And our love will always last
Yes, I hear the doorbell ringing
Why does time fly past

A Song Of Love

You composed a song of love
Dedicated just to me
Placed me high on your pedestal
For all the world to see

How those words haunt me
They touched deep in my soul
Instead of reaching between your lines
I lost all control

In your eyes I held the world
But let it slip away
Now I've only memories
A lonely price to pay

Hunger

I was feeling so hungry
No food could satisfy
Each man looked the same
Just another guy

Then, as if like an alien, you appeared
As though from outer space
Could we have met before?
Another time or place

Your eyes looked in mine
Just melted my frost
I felt as though I'd arrived
For so long have I been lost

That feeling of excitement
When you touched my hand
Things that were so commonplace
I couldn't understand

With you it was so different
Like a new chapter in my book

Wait For Me

I'm here my love
You're there
Do you ever think?
Do you still care?

The wonder of your arms
The softness of your kiss
All these moments
We both have missed

Though in your eyes
They seemed to say
Wait for me love
We'll be together one day

Us Two

My last words will be for you
My last picture will be of us two
If here on Earth, we cannot be
Will be together, in Heaven eternally

I'd love to feel your soul in me
To make a son for all to see
Our love will grow and burn forever
We'll always forever be together

Morning

I had rehearsed a line in my mind
When the time was right
Suddenly his lips touched mine
No strength left to fight

In the morning I woke early
Just gazed into his face
Surely this can't be true
It must be another time and place

I softly kissed his face
He awoke and held me tight
Telling me for the first time he'd found love
This really felt right

Suddenly the phone rang
He said he'd have to go
Begging me to stay right there
When he'd be back, he didn't know

Time moves so quickly
True love just stands still
You feel numb with cold
Only passion can make you feel

One Love

There will only be one love of my life
This I know for sure
Even if the future serves me rich
My heart will remain poor

To think I really touched my star
Alas, I let you go
Pride does come before a fall
Yes, they told me so

Now my soul warms to visions
That happened so long ago
Burdened with eternal regret
That I didn't let you know

Secret Lover

I have a secret lover
Though different from the rest
We romance on the phone
He puts me to the test

He says how much he wants me
And asks me what I wear
I ask him naughty questions
With him I never care

If I close my eyes
I feel his body close to mine
We never seem to touch
Though the feelings also fine

We promise to meet soon
But never make a date
Don't let's touch reality
Fantasy is our fate

Special Guitar

Like your special guitar
I want to be held in a special way
I want to be caressed like the strings
You so gently play

Longing to be admired
With you there by my side
With you I'll never lose direction
My soul mate, confide.

Loving Feelings

When love begins, the feeling is like
beginning of time
Passion burns the fire bright, the Sun
always shines
Ah, but when the time comes, when the fire
burns less bright
Now the war has begun, battle scenes
ready to fight

The times when eyes would meet, no words
could say more
She calls him selfish, he calls her a bore
So, where does the passion go to die
And if it is no longer our hearts, why do we
cry

It's for the emptiness we feel within
The longing for a new love to begin

June

I feel you want to get close
Though are unsure just like me
Though being that much older
I understand and see

Your words are so impressive
And passion shines out from the rest
Even in a baggy t-shirt and jeans
You make me feel my best

Once or twice I've seen you glance
A look you can't disguise
Were you ever hurt in the past?
Or destroyed by a lover's lies

You don't even know my name,
Or my family tree
Did I reach a part in you,
That only I could see

Car Ride

As I'm riding in your car
The wind blows through my hair
You are sitting here beside me
With a look of loving care

Your fingers gently touch my face
I softly kiss your hand
We do not need words
We just understand

You stop the car and hold me close
My body fills with fire
With your loving I am whole
You conquer my desire

You start the car, I cuddle up
So, warm on your shoulder
Your love fills me with an eternal flame
Never to grow older

The Spinning Wheel

My life was in disarray
I had no direction
Like when an infant child is born
I longed for affection

People spoke, their words rang out
Run and hide, try not to shout
My life just span, like a spinning wheel
An endless nightmare, nothing was real

Suddenly the world stopped
I looked into your eyes
You wooed my soul
And coloured my skies

You warm my passion
With endless fire
A fantasy lover
I'll always desire

Wishing Star

Wishing star, make my dreams come true
Bring my love once more
Then I was young and insecure
This time I know I'm sure

All those years ago
You made any dream come true
For when our eyes first met
It's as though he also knew

Could he still wish upon your star,
Or has his passion gone?
I only knew he wooed my soul,
And together we belong

Naughty Woman

Love of my life come share my desire
Fill my soul with your passion and fire
Make me feel just like a woman should
Sometimes naughty, sensual and good

Lay me down on your bed, day and night
Everlasting love, like an endless fight
Hold me high on your pedestal through life
I will then be mother, lover, friend and wife

Exotic Meal

As I eat his exotic meal
Our eyes will slowly meet
Later he'll read me his latest lyrics
And run his fingers through my hair
Making me feel like Heaven
Without those wings to wear

Now I'm cosy in bed
With that one person to read my book
Well, it just has to be Bamber Gascoigne
I don't have to look!
Well, you can tell the communication
between the lines
In reality, I'm a fulltime strawberry wine!

Love and kisses, Susan Ealey

I Can't Follow You

No, I will not follow you
With your waiting hand
Yes, I'm also tempted
Though try to understand

We feel so physical for each other
And passion could run high
Now you look at me with waiting eyes
Begging me to try
Oh, it would be easy to kiss and feel your
arms
Seeing how you want me
It's hard to resist your charms

Please listen, for deep down inside me
I feel it's also wrong
We both have such heavy commitments
Like me you must be strong

You tell me I'm so different,
And together we must be
Don't you know it's just a dream,
Can't you see?

I know I'll always wonder, yes, and regret
Though that passion will always scare my
heart
That day when we met

Three Little Words

Funny how words can let you down
Though millions can fill a dictionary
I still wear a frown

Just three little words as simple as could be
Would have said it all
How silly of me

I love you
I need you
Come be mine
Without you by my side
There is no sunshine

Far Away In Time

I long for you to kiss my lips, so my heart
can skip a beat
Call me on the telephone, plan a
rendezvous where we can meet
Come and look into my eyes, feel my
heated fire
Alone I'm cold as stone, Venus without
desire
I've so much passion and fire, which lies
barren in my soul
You are the love of my life, my destiny, my
goal

That old familiar nightmare, where only fools
dare tread
No waking release, like in a dream, only
reality instead
Familiar faces, with voices that sound the
same to me
Funny how I search for your eyes, to come
and set me free
Only a fool would turn away, when destiny
shows a hand
If only you would give me a chance, to
explain and understand

Have I learnt my final lesson, ready to pass
the test
Can I now hold my head high, and believe
I'm the best

Different shaped faces, their voices all
sound the same
Now I can see their disguises, finally I've
learnt the game
Only a gullible fool, would fall for such a line
I feel one step above them, so far away in
time

Part Time Lover

I want you for my lover
Though not for all time
Tell me how you want me
And long to be mine

Longing to feel your passion
Just come light my fire
Let me be your fantasy
Your wish is my desire

I'll never ask those questions
So, you'll have no need to lie
Just don't leave me cold
If I'm not free, I'll fly

My Kinda Guy

My, isn't he gorgeous, just look at his smile
He's the kinda guy, I'd like to stay a while

True he can have the pick of any cherries in
the bowl
Wow, how those eyes woo my soul

Yes, I know he's younger, though it's that
innocent look
I long for him to treat me, as his very special
book

Each page he can caress, and read with
great care
I'd teach a woman's needs, and the way
she longs to share

Hey, he's looking at me, do you think he can
tell?
I'd give up all my worldly goods, just to feel
his fire in Hell

Light My Eyes

Come light my eyes
With your passion and fire
Fill my soul
With your constant desire

Possess and keep me locked in your heart
Touch my lips with yours, make our story
start

Lie down with me
Your body close to mine
Make me feel a woman
Sensual and divine

When morning comes
Run your fingers through my hair
Our life will be of love
Fantasy and care

So, come open your eyes
And look into mine
For I'll be your woman
Till the end of time

When We Met

How often do I think back,
To when we met
Like a romantic scene from a movie,
How could I forget

Your eyes met mine, you lit my fire, all the
world stood still
I tried to look away from you, the feeling
was quite unreal
How could a stranger look at me, and make
me feel so good
But then as the evening wore on, I think I
understood

For love in our lifetime
We search for the special mate
Yes, you are the only man for me
My destiny and fate

So many sweet moments
Of memories in the past
You lit the passion in my soul
My love will always last

The Letter

Dear kind Sir, this is a letter I cannot send
Just a few lines to say I love you
Wishing you were my friend

How is life with you now?
Are days sunny and bright?
Or do you still wake up,
Wishing in darkness of the night

I hear you've been drifting
From tinsel town to shores
Though your fame is over-flowing
Is your heart still poor?

Well I close now, wishing you health and
happiness too
Oh PS: I just can't get over you

You I See

Hey, don't you know
It's you I see when I feel so lost
Memories and thoughts combine
Yes, I've paid the cost

Your handsome face, warm smile
And those eyes so blue
To think we almost reached our star
If only it was true

Why, why, didn't I tell you?!!
Those words I longed to say
I played the part of a fool
Acting in a play

Word and pictures spent with you,
Often fill my mind
You made me feel so special,
You were so very kind

You placed me on your pedestal
And sang a song for me
I'll never get over you
Find and set me free
For I love you so deeply,
How it hurts to say your name
Why did I treat the love of my life,
Like a childish game

Knowledge & Knowing

This passion inside keeps right on growing
Like time with age, knowledge and knowing
It's like a passion for your desire and need
Not sure of an answer but filled with greed
What do I deserve, love, beast or friend?
Someone to excite, or a lover to the end?

June 21

Can't we be just good friends?
It's much easier this way
For if you glance the way you do
I'm lost for words to say

Friends have so much fun
And share a secret or two
To become lovers is completely not for me
and you

Yes, I find you make me feel young and
new
Just be a friend and confidant
And I'll always stay true

Past Chapter

When days are in limbo
And darkness shows no peace of mind
I search back in my memory
Until once again I find

Those moments we shared together
Which warms my very soul
I reminisce the way our eyes met
And my passion found its goal

Yes, it's a past chapter in my life
Many pages have since been passed
No matter how I try to erase them
My love will always last

VOLUME 4
Space Lady

Man V Machine

This is the twentieth century, where men
have reached the Moon
We have home-made computers, learn too
much too soon

Our children grow so quickly
Painted faces, shaven heads
Why it only seemed like yesterday,
We kissed them to bed

Brilliant minds worked together
It substituted Man for machine
Factory offices are bare now
Where once faces were seen

Father Christmas

Will Father Christmas visit me again this
year?
His eyes full of wonderment, his smile all a
cheer

What presents will he bring me
Oh, I can't wait to see
Of course, he'll have to visit other children
before me

Perhaps this time I'll see him
And his reindeers flying through the sky and
snow
Oh, Mummy, will I ever see him, will I ever
know
For I've heard older children, say it's just a
silly fairy-tale
Just like Jonah, who lived in a whale

Though Father Christmas will always visit
me
For without my Old Santa, what would
Christmas be?

Winter To Spring

Winter turns to spring leaves
Turn a brighter shade
Daffodils start to bloom
From small seeds they were made

Birds start to sing loud
They've come home to rest
Each busy collecting twigs and leaves
For their homing nest

Mornings longer, darker evenings, turn to
light
The air has a smell of sweetness
In the dark shadow of night

Spring fresh, spring when everything shines
new
When lovers seem to fall, under a sky of
blue

The Courtroom

She walked into the courtroom
Eyes wide and full of fear
Gazing in their direction
I could almost feel her tear

Everything was ready for the story to begin
Her life would now be an open book
Ending in such sin

People rose as the judge walked,
Amongst the counsels hurried speech
We sat down obediently,
Like back in a classroom he'd come to
teach

The Café

She sat in a café, grey hair and cloudy eyes
Drew at her cigarette, between heavy sighs
Just another lonely person, passing the time
My, how cruel this world is, it really is a
crime

Then her eyes looked up, to see me staring
down
I tried to turn away, but she caught me in
her frown
Her face suddenly softened, and broke into
a smile
Please her voice was asking me, sit and
stay a while

I know I look quite strange, but that is what
age can do
Though believe these grey days, were once
always blue
You see I must have been your age, the
ideal model wife
The war inside was growing, for me to
change my life

So many, many times, I'd let temptation
pass me by
All those lonely memories, how I used to cry

June 1984

That same old haunted feeling, as someone
passes too near
Shared with a shaking in my soul, that
cannot hide any fear

It can happen in a subway crossing
Or a busy shopping street
Never knowing what eyes are staring
Or when again you meet

Funny you never think it can happen to you
How cruel fate can be
Though when it does, your freedom is gone
No longer are you free

When there is nothing left, not even a smile
each day
You know the end has come, there's
nothing left to stay
The bills, predictability, now you can no
longer bear
A contract with names on, nothing left to
share

Solicitors, strange buildings, loom large in
your mind
You have to fight hard for your freedom
A new life yet to find

The Bomb

Shutters on windows, shutters on doors
The bomb is on its way
No time to think about shopping
Get the children in from play

Make sure you have your supplies
Ready for your shelter in the ground
There to stay in solitary
Hoping to be found

When days and nights have passed
With courage to peer outside to find
There's not a trace of the world you knew
How God can be unkind

Just an evil mist
Seems like the end of time
No more to walk through fields of green
Or to feel the sunshine

You will search for an answer
What has all this achieved?
A disagreement that's past history
Just to satisfy their greed

Autumn To Winter

As autumn leaves break gently
And fall softly to the ground
The birds sing a final farewell
Before their final sound

Damp and smoky winter nights
Where a fire feels so warm and new
I look into your eyes of love
And know our love is true
Happy Winter's Birthday my true love

Strange Light

As I peered out my window
A strange light caught my eye
It was aimed to the Moon and stars
That light our evening sky

I shook my head, rubbed my eyes,
Oh no, it's coming near
Trying to shout, I was numbed through with
novice fear

What happened next you won't believe
To me it's still a dream
The universe is not barren
Life is not what it seems

Somehow, I boarded their ship
For I was seated in a large green seat
Strange noises greeted my eyes
Their master I was to meet

Yellow eyes, shaven heads,
Features that seemed similar to mine
Funny how when one is nervous,
You look to find the time

The Tramp

He stood there by the corner
Looking sad and forlorn
Clothes that didn't fit quite right
Shabby and torn

Was he young or old?
It was really hard to tell
Oh, that cold look in his eyes
A prisoner of Hell

A bottle in his hand
He swayed from side to side
Praying he would not see me
There's nowhere to hide

Well, aren't you the pretty one! he shouted,
Hands reaching out for me
I turned around trapped in his gaze
I couldn't break free

His voice suddenly stiffened
As though to confuse us all
Letting go of my arm
Stood up, straight and tall

Yes, I'm a freak!
Don't smell too good I know!
I've been to Hell and back many times,
Yet still no scars to show

I was still afraid to speak

Afraid of what he might say
Though still he held me in his gaze
With words of an unknown day

Then quite suddenly, he slumped against
the wall
Once again, the drunk, the nuisance and
fool
It was just another day, just another face
How life can be so cruel, to make one lose
their place

Up Above

Is there a God up there?
Do I speak alone?
Do I have a spirit?
Or has it left to roam

Wishing Star

Wishing star in the sky
Can't you hear my plea?
I've been talking to you every night
Can't you hear me??

When I look out my window at night
I see the stars so shiny and bright
Some are big, some are small
Look at these blue ones, over the wall

Then I look up
At the beautiful Moon
It shines so bright
And yet goes so soon

Old Faces

Why do old people seem to look and act the same?
Faces which show the lives of laughter, tears and pain
Where once their bodies walked straight and proud
Now seem smaller with voices harsh though not loud

To think their hearts were filled with love and passion
What games did they play to match their fashion?
Some just sit in a chair all day, watch the clouds go by
Theirs go back to Memory Lane, and try hard not to cry

Granddads' talk of past wars, and how things are today
Grannies' sit and knit, whilst their grandchildren play
Each one has played their role, each different from the rest
One day it will be our turn, to face that final test

Astral Plane

Searching in my astral plane
Alone and so unsure
Wealth is just a no
My passion empty and poor

I'm told I belong to a family
Yet an alien to their touch
How they hate and accuse me
I long to belong so much

An unsolved jigsaw puzzle
Missing places lost in time
An unsolved painting
Faces so unkind

Have I returned to Earth
To fulfil an unknown guest
It would explain the emotions I live
That served under a test
So here I stand, a lover
Searching for a sign ahead

London

To smell pollution in the air
To see a pigeon fly over Trafalgar Square
To catch a tube on the Circle Line
To walk through Regent's Park with sunshine
To feel the rush passing by
London still brings a tear to my eye

Birds In Flight

I look down from my window
And see the birds in flight
The way they crowd my back yard
Like Trafalgar Square, well, not quite

Blackbirds, sparrows, robins,
All seem to fight for crumbs
I make sure I throw plenty,
Enough for everyone

Then in different directions they fly home,
To their nest and young
Feeling full and tired,
For their supper they have sung

If I dare forget you,
Know you'll come pecking on my door

Mother Earth

God made us strong like Mother Earth
Complete with a womb to give birth

Our hands are strong, to clean and care
Bodies that are warm, to give and share

Though what about our minds?
What happens to them?
When we are alone
Locked in our domestic den

Get Ready For War

The battleships are near,
With planes ready to fly
Will it be the time,
To kiss our world goodbye

Young soldiers at the ready,
Guns in their hand
They talk and sing triumph,
When they reach land

Oh, little do they know,
Of blood and hate to come
Or of the grief of mothers,
Never to see their sons

Winter

Winters cold breeze touches my face
And then I think of you
I board the train for another workday
Wondering if you knew

Same chair, same desk,
Life goes round and round
Trying to black out visions
My mind still hears the sound

My life's caught in a chapter
Unable to break free

Space Lady

I am a space lady, in charge of the sky
In my supersonic suit, and bionic eye

My name will be in history books
I've badges on my chest
When my electronics wear out
I'll be burned with the best

I do not desire a man, he is no good to me
I have no womb inside, a mother I'll never
be
Women have spoken of fantasies
When I was based on Earth
Stories of lovers and desire to give birth

They stared at me with sorrow, they just
don't seem to see
My only master, my fantasy, is me

A Christmas Day

Once upon a Christmas Day, not so long
ago
I awoke early and I did spy Santa in the
snow
Carrying loads of special gifts
Which were loaded on his sledge
I climbed onto my windowsill
To see Rudolph's pushing head

I shut my eyes so tightly,
And Santa tiptoed into my room
Then he said in a soft voice,
Enjoy your gifts my little friend
For Christmas is over too soon

Merry Christmas

I Want To Be Mae West

I want to be in the movies,
Be like Mae West
Be a whole lotta woman,
Give my best

People will come from miles around, and
travel far
Just to see this rising star
Leading men of Hollywood, will want me for
a date
I will star as Jane in *Tarzan, and his Mate*

A beautiful mansion in Hollywood Hills
Have expensive parties, which cost a
thousand-dollar bills

Get married to a prince or a millionaire
Live a life of luxury without a care
And when my chin gets double
And my eyes need a lift
Get yourself a real human
You deserve a gift!

Spring To Fall

Another spring, another fall
When autumn leaves turn brown
My eyes shade a misty grey
A head burdened with a frown

Young lovers kiss goodnight
Where a full Moon warms their embrace
I too had warmth in my heart
Until you left without a trace

Young or old, black or white
We all have a lesson which we're taught
Soldiers dressed in uniform
Wars still to be fought

The Dentist

I have to visit the dentist tomorrow
Have a filling so I'm told
Mummy says don't be afraid
Be strong and bold
What if he takes my front teeth out?
A gap for all to see
How my friends will laugh
And say nasty rhymes to me

Perhaps I'll have to wear false ones?
Take them out at night
Just like Granny does
Which gives me a fright!
I can imagine he'll be standing there
That needle in his hand
The nurse will be holding me down
In case I want to stand

Still I'll have the afternoon off
To play with soldiers and toys
I won't have to study hard
Like the other boys
Perhaps the dentist visit won't be bad after
all?
Until I'm in the waiting room, and my name
they will call

Super Idol

Here you stand upon the stage, looking all
so good
Singing songs of love making, young girls
feel like they should
When you smile, their fantasies seem to
come true
You are their super idol, turn their grey to
blue

Pictures hang upon walls, you smile just for
them
I guess you know how a lion feels, trapped
within his den
You have fame and fortune, your every wish
come true
Though without your freedom, can you see
this through?

Rock Concert

I was at a rock concert
A face in the crowd
The music really touched my soul
I longed to cry out loud

Then the loud tempo stopped
A quiet ballad began
About a woman empty inside
Who one day finds her man

Success

Well hello, success has changed you, or is it
just your shell?
You still have a hunger in your eyes, only I
can tell
Travelling this global world, a hit in every
town
Remember those all-night parties, you
played the painted clown
Oh yes, I read those stories, are they really
true?
Now when I hear your songs, it makes me
shine blue

The Bus Stop

I'm standing at the bus stop
The rain is pouring down
With cars splashing at my legs
No wonder I wear a frown
Twenty minutes I've stood helpless!!!

Your Voice

Your voice seems to touch me, right down
in my soul
Making me wish you were with me, to lose
all control
Each track from your album, seems like an
episode from my life
Making me forget, I'm the regimental wife

Even in my teens
When I was young and fancy free
No other band can compare
To the way you stimulate and excite me

Just five handsome faces
So much younger than I
You make my spirits rise
With thoughts again to fly

Steve Wright Radio DJ

Dear 'Steve Wright in the Afternoon'
I think you are an adorable crazy loon!
At first, I tried to shut my eyes,
From your constant trail
Even played record and tapes,
Though to no avail

Your humour played me
So, I turned you on
Just gave in and know when you're going
naughty,
In the middle of a song

Clean kitchen mugs and start potato peeling
What's going on down there?! My boys
shout, and bang upon my ceiling
Oh, its only Mother freaking out!
Steve Wright's on you see
I have another barmy life
You share a birthday with me

Yes, he is so intellectual, and good looking
too
I once shared this question, I'm a happy
condemned fool
So just keep up your patter
It really helps me laugh all the time
A big thank you, with a glass of wine!

Handsome Hero

So, my handsome hero
Where do you go to rest?
When you no longer have to shine your ego
When you've done your best

The pretty ladies have all gone home
You no longer have to impress
You can be yourself now
You've truly past the test

And when you take a new escort out,
So pretty on your arm
Do you excel yourself,
When you kick to catch your charm

Or do you long to have a woman,
Who'll love you as you are
The man behind the image,
Of the bored pop star

Headlines

The words they printed in the newspaper
Seemed so large it shook my mind
Could this really be the man I loved?
Who I trusted, yet I look to find

Every loving detail of that past chapter we
spent
How I used to pose nude, just to pay our
rent
Arguments, heated fights, which ended up
in bed
Oh, Christ how can you do this?! I wish I
was dead

Pin Up

I've fallen in love with a boy
And the way he sleeps so fine
I love the make-up that he wears
His dress I wish was mine
His make-up is so perfect
Hair falling round his face
I would never ever hurt him
It would be a disgrace

Ideal Man Part 1

My ideal man is so complex, just like me I
suppose
He would have Simon Le Bon's sexy eyes,
and Ian Botham's nose
Harrison Ford's bodyworks, with Bamber
Gascoigne's voice
Yes, they are my fantasy, my very own
choice

Ideal Man Part 2

Oh, to be awoken by John Taylor
With his brown eyes and sensual smile
He'd butter me hot
And woo me for a while

Then around 11.30 Ian Botham would call
for us to play our own test
With lip gloss and slinky hot pants, I'm sure
to play my best

The Unknown Fan

It was just like a wish come true
My own fantasy dream
Life is full of lessons
Not always as it seems

I was just an unknown fan
In love with you like the rest
Until I was called backstage after your
concert
Put before your test

At first, I couldn't speak
Well, my legs trembled so
Feeling like the number 1 loon
Longing to escape, just go

You gently kissed my hand
Poured me a cool glass of wine
Telling me I outshone the rest
How I really looked fine

At last my voice found my mouth
We hit it off so well
Little knowing in your brand-new saloon
We travelled first class to Hell

You wined and dined me
Then danced the night away
As we parked at your apartment
Waiting eyes, asked me to stay

Was I still in a dream?
Could this really be happening to me?
I was with a number 1 idol
Oh, why couldn't he let me be

Autumn

Autumn comes, with the windy rain and chill
The Sun still shines, though the heat you no
longer feel

Evenings draw in quicker, a blanket covers
the sky
Flowers and roses, cast their petals and die

Cheeks are rosy, noses are red
Winter draws on, as we tuck cosy into bed

Writing

I sit down to write
The thoughts run through my head
Paper at the ready
Why the pen feels like lead

It seems the words,
I need to express on this paper of mine
Will be written one day,
In another space in time

Susan Ealey, A Woman's Verse

I love you always
I miss my best friend
I'll do you proud
So, when you look over me
Which I know you do
You'll smile your beautiful smile
Love you forever Mum

Matthew-John xxxxx

Christmas Eve 2019

Printed in Poland
by Amazon Fulfillment
Poland Sp. z o.o., Wrocław

54425651R00108